Your Plants

Plain and Practical Directions for the Treatment of Tender and Hardy Plants in the House and in the Garden

James Sheehan

CHAPTER I.

HOW TO MAKE A LAWN.

A smooth lawn is a great attraction of itself, even if there is not a tree or shrub upon it. When it is once made, a lawn is easily kept in order, yet we seldom see a good one. There are three things to be taken into consideration in securing a fine lawn. First, location; Second, quality of the soil; Third, the kinds of seed to be sown.

LOCATION.

This is the most important matter relating to a good lawn. In selecting a site upon which to build, not the least consideration should be the possibility of having a fine lawn, one that will cost as little as possible to keep in a nice and attractive condition. The nearer level the land is, the better. If a house is built on an elevation back from the road, a sloping lawn has a good effect. Where the land is rolling and hilly, it should be graded into successive terraces, which, though rather expensive, will look well. Low lands should be avoided as much as possible in selecting a site on which it is intended to make a good lawn. Low land can be improved by thorough under-drainage. If the land is wet on which we design making a lawn, we should first thoroughly underdrain it by laying tiles two rods apart, and two feet below the surface. Large-growing trees should never be planted on the lawn, grass will not thrive under them. Fruit trees, like the apple, cherry, and peach, are exceedingly out of place on a fine lawn. The finest yard we ever saw had not a tree on it that exceeded ten feet in hight. Flowering shrubs, low-growing evergreens, a few weeping and deciduous trees of moderate size, with flower-beds neatly planted, make an attractive door-yard.

SOIL.

This is the mother of all vegetation. Nothing, not even grass, will flourish on a poor soil. The quality of the soil varies in different localities. We often find a fine sward on a stiff clay soil, and also on a light gravelly one. The soil best adapted to the growth of a good sward, is a sandy loam with a gravelly bottom. In making new lawns, there is sometimes more or less grading to be done, and often where a knoll has been cut off the sub-soil is exposed, and it will not do to sow the seed upon these patches until the spots have been thoroughly covered with manure which is to be worked in. If a new lawn of any extent is to be made, it should first be plowed deep, and if uneven and hilly, grade it to a level surface. The surface should have a heavy dressing of manure, which should be lightly plowed under, and then the surface should be dragged several times until fine, and then rolled with a heavy roller. The seed may now be sown, after which it should be rolled again. The spring is the best time to do this work, although if the fall be dry, it will answer nearly as well to do it at that time. The dryer the ground in preparing it for the seed, and for the sowing of the same, the better. In preparing a small plot of ground for a lawn, the spade, hand-rake, and small roller may be used in place of the larger implements.

SEED.

Much difficulty is often experienced in obtaining a good mixture of grass seed for the lawn, and different mixtures are recommended and sold for sowing lawns, some of which are entirely worthless. Great pains should be taken to have nothing but first-class seeds, which should be obtained direct of some responsible dealer. The finest sward we ever saw was made from the following mixture:

- 10 quarts Rhode Island Bent-grass.
- 4 quarts White Clover.
- 8 quarts Kentucky Blue-grass.
- 6 quarts Red-top Grass.

Sow at the rate of six bushels to the acre. Grass seed can be sown in the fall any time from the first of October to the first of December. If the seed be sound, a good sward may be expected the following summer, and a good turf may be expected from spring sown seeds if the season is not too dry.

The dryer the ground is when the seeds are sown, the better. To keep the lawn in a flourishing condition, fresh and green all summer, it will need a top-dressing of well-rotted manure applied in the fall, at least once every two years. Grass roots derive their nourishment close to the surface, hence the great advantage of top-dressing. In some localities where the frost "heaves" the sod to any extent during the winter, it will be advantageous to roll it down in the spring with a heavy roller, doing it just after a heavy rain. When the ground is soft and pliable, this will make the surface smooth, and in proper condition for the lawn-mower to pass over it.

Frequent mowing will thicken the sward. It is not necessary to sow oats, as some do, to shade the ground until the seeds have started, that is an "old fogy" notion, and is now obsolete.

CHAPTER II.

SOIL FOR POTTING.—ARTIFICIAL FERTILIZERS.

Good, fresh, rich soil, is an element that is indispensable to the growth of healthy, vigorous plants. A plant cannot be thrifty if grown in soil that has become musty and stale with long continued use; it must have fresh soil, at least once a year.

Perhaps the best soil for general potting purposes, and the kind most extensively used by florists, is a mixture of equal parts of decayed sods, and well-rotted stable manure, and occasionally, especially if the sod is clayey, a little sand is added. The sods for this purpose may be obtained from along the road-side, almost anywhere, while good stable manure is always readily obtainable. Select some out-of-the-way place in the lot, or garden, and gather the sods in quantity proportioned to the amount of potting to be done. Lay down a course of the sods, and on top of this, an equal course of well-rotted manure, and so on, alternately, until the heap is finished; the last layer being sod. This heap should be turned over carefully, two or three times a year, breaking up the sods finely with a spade, or fork. The whole mass will become thoroughly mixed, rotted, and fit for use in a year from the time the heap was made. For those who have a large number of plants, we think it will pay to adopt this method of preparing soil for them, instead of purchasing it of the florist at twenty-five cents or more per bushel. Some florists sport a great variety of different soils, which are used in the growing of plants of different natures, requiring, as they claim, particular kinds of soil.

Whatever of truth, if any, there is in this view, it has never been demonstrated to our mind. All kinds of plants have a common requirement in respect to soil, and the differences in growth of various species is attributable to climate and other causes than that of soil. At least that has been our experience.

ARTIFICIAL FERTILIZERS.

This question is frequently asked! Do you recommend the use of artificial fertilizers for house plants, and does it benefit them? I invariably answer yes, if used judiciously. The use of good special fertilizers will help the growth of some kinds of plants, which, without such aid, would scarcely meet our expectations. The term artificial fertilizers, applies to all manurial applications, save those produced by domestic animals.

I have always believed, however, that when any fertilizer is needed, good, well-rotted stable-manure should have the preference over all artificial fertilizers. Where this manure cannot be readily obtained, or used conveniently, then special fertilizers can be employed as substitutes with good results. In applying manure in the liquid form to plants, use an ounce of guano to every gallon of water, and apply it to those plants that are in a healthy growing condition, about once every two weeks. It is a mistake to try to stimulate into growth, by the use of fertilizers, those plants which give every indication of being sickly or stunted; they will make such a plant sicker, if they do not kill it outright. If guano is used in potting soil, it should be in the proportion of one pound to every bushel of soil.

CHAPTER III.

SELECTING AND SOWING SEEDS.

All individuals of the vegetable world are so created as to reproduce themselves from seed or its equivalent. Every plant that grows seems to possess the power to perpetuate its kind. All kinds of flowering plants can be grown from the seed, providing good, sound seeds are obtained, and they are placed under the proper influences to make them germinate and grow.

The amateur cultivator has many difficulties to contend with in raising plants from seed. Some times it is difficult to obtain pure, sound seeds, but these should always be secured if possible, taking great pains in selecting varieties, and in obtaining them of some reliable dealer. If we sow seeds, and they fail to germinate, our first thought is to censure the dealer or raiser of the seed for lack of integrity in his business, while in reality the fault may be our own, and due to careless sowing.

Those who raise seed for the market take great pains to produce none but good, sound seeds, and in nine cases out of ten, where seeds fail to germinate and grow, the fault is with those who sow them, and not on account of poor quality of seed. This we know from experience.

Three things are absolutely essential in the sowing of seeds, in order to have that success which we all desire to attain:

First; care should be taken to obtain fresh, pure seeds, without which all our after work with them will be in vain.

Second; the soil in which to sow them should be a fine, mellow loam, free from stones and other coarse materials.

Thirdly; sowing the seed. The general custom is to sow in drills. The depth at which seeds should be sown must of course be regulated according to their fineness, or coarseness.

Seeds that are exceptionally fine, like those of Lobelias, Petunias, Ferns, and other very tiny seeds, ought never to be covered deeper than the sixteenth of an inch, with very fine soil sifted on them through a fine sieve; the soil should then be lightly patted down with the back of a shovel. This will prevent the seeds from shriveling before they start to germinate.

Seeds like those of the Pansy, Verbena, etc., require a covering of a quarter to a half inch of soil, while those like the Nasturtium, Ricinus, etc., may be covered to the depth of an inch.

The regular florist has facilities for raising plants from seed that most amateurs do not possess, but we will give a few suggestions that will enable those who desire to start their own plants, to do it successfully by the aid of the directions here given.

A cheap and simple method is, to take four plain boards, of an equal length, say three feet long, and ten inches deep, and nail together to form a square frame. Then place this frame upon a bed of rich soil, prepared for the purpose in some sheltered, warm spot. The bed should be just wide enough to be enclosed within the frame. Within this enclosure sow your seeds, and cover with a glass sash. Seeds can be started in March in this frame, and afford plants for setting out in April and May.

A bank of earth, or manure, may be thrown around the outside of the frame to keep it snug and warm. After sowing the seed in this frame, shade it for four or five days by placing a cloth over the sash, this will prevent too much heat and light until the seeds have commenced to germinate, after which it can be removed without injury.

CHAPTER IV.

MAKING AND PLANTING FLOWER-BEDS.

People of the present day can scarcely be contented with tall, waving timothy in the front door-yard, and the rickety board-fence that enclosed a scene of almost primitive rusticity—the state of things in our "forefathers' days."

In place of the timothy growing to hay in the front yard, we now see fine, smoothly-cut lawns of refreshing greenness; and fences of pickets, wire, and rustic iron, have supplanted the ancient board fences. In place of the tall-growing Sunflower and Hollyhock that sprung up here and there at random, we now see beds of choice and beautiful flowers artistically arranged and carefully cultivated by loving hands.

All is system now about the door-yard and premises, where once were neglect and confusion.

Every home should have one or more beds planted with attractive flowers. It would be a difficult matter to give specific instructions as to planting these beds, as every one has his own peculiar tastes in such matters, which is sometimes governed by surroundings, locality, etc.

There are some general rules however, observed by gardeners in planting flower-beds that it would be well to observe.

The following notes on planting flower-beds were handed us some time ago. We do not know the name of the writer, but have strong reason to believe them to be from the pen of the late James Vick.

"There are a great variety of opinions as regards the most effective way of planting flower-beds. Some prefer to mix plants of different colors and varieties, others prefer the ribbon-style of planting, now so generally in use in Europe. If the promiscuous style is adopted, care should be taken to dispose the plants in the beds, so that the tallest will be at the back of the bed; if the leader is against a wall or background of shrubbery, the others should graduate to the front, according to the hight. In open beds, on the lawn, the tallest plants should be in the centre, the others grading down to the front, on all sides, interspersing the colors so as to form the most effective contrast in shades.

"But for grand effect, nothing, in our estimation, can ever be obtained in promiscuous planting, to equal that resulting from planting in masses, or ribbon lines. In Europe lawns are cut so as to resemble rich, green velvet; on these the flower-beds are laid out in every style one can conceive of; some are planted in masses of blue, yellow, crimson, white, etc., separate beds of each harmoniously blended on the carpeting of green.

"Then again, the ribbon-style is used in large beds, in forms so various that allusion can here be made to only a few of the most conspicuous. In a circular bed, say twenty feet in diameter, the bordering can be made of blue Lobelia, attaining a hight of six inches; next plant Mrs. Pollock Geranium, or Bijou Zonal Geraniums, growing about nine inches high. If you plant Mrs. Pollock, on the next row to it plant Mountain of Snow (silvered-leaved geranium), next a circle of Red Achyranthes; there are several varieties of this plant. Next Centaurea candidissima (Dusty Miller); the centre being a mound of Scarlet Salvias.

"Narrow beds along the margins of walks can be formed of low-growing plants, such as the White Lobelia, Gypsophila, or Silvered Alyssum, for the front line, followed next by the Tom Thumb Tropæolum; then as a centre, or third line, Fuchsia Golden Fleece; as a second margined-line on the other side, Silver-leaved Geraniums with scarlet flowers, followed by a line of blue Lobelia.

"Shaded stars have a fine effect on a lawn; cut a star and plant it with either Verbenas, Petunias, Phlox Drummondii, or Portulaca. The ends of the stars should be white, and shaded to the centre."

A whole volume might be written on the subject of gardening, without exhausting its variety or interest, but we take it for granted that our readers will exercise their own tastes, or call on some competent gardener to give advice in the premises.

CHAPTER V.

WATERING PLANTS.—IS COLD WATER INJURIOUS?

Probably the most important matter to be observed in growing house-plants is that of watering them. The cultivator should know just when to water, and to give it where it will do the most good. Amateur florists often exhibit much poor judgment in watering. It is the habit of some to keep the soil about their plants constantly soaked with water, and they wonder why they are not thrifty or healthy. These cultivators do not stop to consider that such treatment is unnatural, and will have an effect contrary to what is desired. There are those who resort to the opposite extreme, and keep their plants all the time in a perishing condition of dryness, which is even worse than if they were watered to death. If we will observe how judiciously Nature distributes the sunshine and shadow, the periodical rains, and the refreshing dews, we will learn an important lesson. A pot, or other receptacle in which plants are grown, should be porous; glazed, or painted pots, ought never to be used, where plain, unglazed pots can be obtained; all non-porous pots of tin and similar material, should be discarded. Plants growing in them can never compare in health with those that have the advantage of plain porous pots. There should be a hole of sufficient size in the bottom of each pot, to allow the water to drain off, and to pass away as soon as possible. Placing a few pieces of broken crocks, or charcoal, in the bottom of the pots will facilitate a rapid drainage, as good drainage is essential to the growth of strong, and healthy plants. When plants require water, it will be indicated by a light, dry appearance of the top of the soil, and if watered when in this condition, it will do the most good. Give water only when in this condition, and then copiously, giving them all they will soak up at the time, then withhold water until the same indication of their want of it again appears, then apply it freely. Unless plants are in a very dry atmosphere, as in a warm parlor in winter, they will seldom require watering. In summer they should be closely watched, and if exposed to wind and sun, they will require daily watering, to keep them in a flourishing state. When plants are suffering from drouth, it will be indicated by the drooping of the leaves, and they will frequently turn yellow, and drop off prematurely; this can be avoided by timely attention each day.

In summer, watering in the cool of the evening will be followed by the best results, for it will give the plants time to take up and assimilate the moisture necessary to their life, and being completely charged with water, they will be prepared for the hot sun and drying winds of the following day.

IS COLD WATER INJURIOUS TO PLANTS?

Those who study works on horticulture by different writers, will discover many opposing views in respect to the modes of caring for, and the treatment of plants. The proper temperature for water when applied to plants, has been frequently discussed by different writers; some contend that cool water, just drawn from a well or cistern, should never be showered upon plants, but that it should first be heated to the temperature of the room in which the plants are standing. Others, with equal zeal, claim that cold water will not injure the plants in the least, contending that the water will assume the right temperature before injury is done the plant. Now which is right? We have experimented in this matter to a considerable extent, in order to satisfy ourselves as to which of these two views is correct. In the month of December I took from my collection twelve large geraniums and placed them by themselves in the conservatory; six of these I watered with cold water, drawn from a hydrant pipe at the temperature of 45°, and the other six were supplied with water from a barrel standing in the conservatory, and was of the same temperature of the house, that is from 60° to 80°. The plants watered with the cold water gave little if any bloom throughout the winter, while the six watered from the barrel grew finely, and bloomed profusely.

Always water your plants in winter time with lukewarm water, if you would have a profusion of flowers, and thrifty-growing plants. The water should be of the same temperature as the room or place where the plants are. There is no theory about it, it is a practical fact, all talk to the contrary notwithstanding.

CHAPTER VI.

ATMOSPHERE AND TEMPERATURE.—INSECTS.

The proper regulation of the atmosphere as to moisture and temperature, is one of the most important points to be observed in cultivating plants in the parlor, or window-garden. Plants will not flourish, bloom, and be healthy, in a dry, dusty atmosphere, even though the best of care otherwise may be bestowed upon them; hence it is that those who attempt to raise plants in their dwellings meet with so little success. There is an immense contrast between the atmosphere of a well regulated green-house and that of an ordinary dwelling. In the green-house, the atmosphere is moist and well-tempered to the healthful growth of plants; while that of the parlor or sitting-room is invariably dry and dusty, and plants will not flourish in it as they would in the conservatory. If the dwelling be heated by coal, there is more or less gas constantly discharged into the air of the room, which is of itself enough to destroy vegetation, or make it sickly. Houses heated by steam, are better adapted to the cultivation of plants.

All plants will not flourish in the common temperature of a living-room; some require a low temperature, and others need a warmer one. The following plants require a temperature of from 70° to 80° in the day-time, and 55° to 60° at night Begonias, Coleuses, Calceolarias, Bouvardias, Ferns (tropical), Hibiscuses, Poinsettias, Tuberoses, Heliotropes, Crotons, Hoyas, Cactuses, all kinds, Caladiums, Cannas, Palms, Orange and Lemon Trees, Geraniums, etc.

The following will do well in an atmosphere ranging from 50° to 60° by day, and 40° to 45° by night: Camellias, Azaleas, Oleanders, Roses, Carnations, Callas, Ivies, Abutilons, Jessamines, Holland-bulbs, Lily-of-the-Valley, Primroses, Violets, Verbenas, Chrysanthemums, etc. Plants will flourish better in the kitchen, where the steam and moisture from cooking are constantly arising, and tempering the atmosphere, than in a dry, dusty sitting-room; hence it is that we find "Bridget" sometimes cultivating a few plants in her kitchen window, that are envied by the mistress of the house, because they are so much finer than those in her parlor or sitting-room.

If a pan of water is set upon a stove in a room where plants are growing, it will help to materially relieve the dryness of the atmosphere. But most all kinds of house-plants will do fairly in a uniform temperature, from 70° by day to 55° by night. Careful observation of the habits and requirements of different kinds of plants, as they come under our care, will greatly assist the cultivator, and in a short time he will be so conversant with their various habits as to know just how to properly treat each and every plant in his collection.

INSECTS UPON PLANTS.

The little green insects so frequently seen on house-plants, are called aphis (plural aphides), plant-lice, or green-fly. They feed upon the tender growth of plants, especially the new leaves, and will rapidly sap and destroy the life of any plant if allowed to remain undisturbed. In the spring these insects abound in great numbers on the plants in green-houses and parlors, or wherever they may be growing, and the remedy should be promptly applied. The greatest enemy to the green-fly is tobacco smoke, made by burning the stems, the refuse of the cigar-maker's shops; allowing the smoke to circulate among the leaves to which the insects are attached, will readily exterminate them. Place the infested plant under a barrel, an ordinary cracker barrel will do, and put under it a pan of burning tobacco, slightly moistened with water. Leave the plant in the smoke for fifteen or twenty minutes, after which remove it. If one "smoking" fails to destroy the insects, repeat the dose three or four times, once each day, until they are completely exterminated.

A strong solution, or "tea," made from soaking tobacco stems in water, and syringing the same over the plants, will effectually destroy the little pests, and not injure the plant in the operation.

CHAPTER VII.

WINTERING PLANTS IN CELLARS.

Many plants, such as Agaves (Century Plants), Oleanders, large Cactuses, etc., that have grown too large to be accommodated in the sitting-room or conservatory; can be successfully wintered in any moderately dry, frost-proof cellar. After placing these large plants in the cellar, it will not be necessary to give them any water, the object being to keep them dormant all winter, which can be done by keeping the soil as dry as possible, but not so dry as to allow the plants to shrivel, or become withered. Large plants of the kinds mentioned, often form desirable ornaments during the summer time, but it is impracticable, in most cases, to bring them into the house in winter, but they can be kept for years by cellaring through the winter as stated. Large Geraniums, Salvia and Heliotrope roots, and even Tea Roses, and Carnations, can be kept moderately well in the cellar by trenching them in dry, or moderately moist sand. Thus many choice specimens of these plants that we are loth to pull up and threw away when winter approaches, can be successfully kept over until the next season. It is a needless expense to purchase a stock of new plants for the garden every year, when we can winter many of the old ones in this simple and inexpensive manner. The leaves of all deciduous plants should be removed before they are put away in this manner. The foliage should remain on the Oleanders and Carnations.

CHAPTER VIII.

THE LAW OF COLOR IN FLOWERS.

The public are so often duped by a set of travelling frauds, who make it their business to represent themselves as being the sole proprietor or agent of some "wonderful" kinds of plants, bulbs, or seeds, which possess the virtue of being remarkably distinct from anything ever seen or heard of before, that many over-credulous ladies or gentlemen fall victims to the unprincipled sharks. Did you ever see any one who could sell rose bushes that would certainly bear blue roses, or plants of the Verbena that produce yellow blossoms, or Tuberose bulbs bearing scarlet flowers? If you have not, you have something to learn, and many have paid dearly for experiences of this kind.

There is a natural law of color in flowers, that the varieties of a species invariably present a certain range of colors. To attempt to introduce a new and distinct color, as for example a blue rose, into a family where the colors are always white, red, and yellow, is an impossibility, and any one who claims to do this, may be set down as a swindler.

Much credit is due Mr. Peter Henderson, an eminent florist and seedsman of New York City, for the vigorous methods employed by him in exposing frauds of this kind, whenever his attention has been called to them. We quote from an article written by Mr. Henderson on this subject, some years ago: "It has long been known among the best observers of such matters, that in certain families of plants, particular colors prevail, and that in no single instance can we ever expect to see blue, yellow, and scarlet colors in varieties of the same species. If any one at all conversant with plants, will bring any family of them to mind, it will at once be seen how undeviating is this law. In the Dahlia we have scarlet and yellow, but no approach to the blue, so in the Rose, Hollyhock, etc. Again in the Verbena and Salvia, we have scarlet and blue, but no yellow. If we reflect, it will be seen that there is nothing out of the order of nature in this arrangement; why then should we expect nature to step outside of what seems to be her fixed laws, and give us a blue rose, etc." A word to the wise, we take it, is sufficient in view of the foregoing facts.

CHAPTER IX.

THE RELATION OF PLANTS TO HEALTH.

Plants at present are more generally cultivated in-doors than formerly, and they may be seen in almost every home. The cultivation of plants in dwellings is decidedly a modern custom—at least to the extent to which it is now practised. One who now contemplates building a dwelling house, plans to have included with the other conveniences of a first-class home, a suitable window for house plants. As the cultivation of plants in dwelling houses increases, the question is raised by some: "Are not plants injurious to health, if growing in the apartments in which we live and sleep?" We know of persons who would not sleep in a room in which a number of plants were growing, giving as the reason that the amount of carbonic acid gas given off by the plants, is detrimental to health. Now this view is either true or it is not true. We have made a particular study of this matter, and speak from experience. Over ten years of my life had been spent in the green-house, among all kinds of plants; I have frequently slept all night among them, and I have never observed it to be in any way detrimental to my health, but, on the contrary, I have never felt better than when among plants. Gardeners, as a class, those who have spent their lives among plants, show, so far as we have observed, a longevity equal to, if not exceeding that of any other class who are engaged in any of the vocations usually regarded as healthy. We must admit, however, that we have never known of a case of chronic rheumatism to be benefited in the least by working in hot-houses, on account of the perpetual dampness of the air. On the other hand, we know of a number of persons afflicted with various other diseases, who have been noticeably benefited by working among plants: perhaps it was owing to the health-giving bodily exercise required by the work, rather than the supposed health-giving effects of the plants themselves; we think the result was due to both. An eminent physician cites a case in which his sister, aged fifty years, was afflicted with tubercular consumption, her death, as the natural result of such a terrible disease being expected at any time, but being an ardent lover of plants and flowers, she was daily accustomed to move among her plants, of which she possessed a large number, in her sleeping room as well as many others in beds outside. Her friends reproved her for sleeping in the same room with her plants; but the years came and went, and she was still found moving among her flowers in her eightieth year, surviving those, who many years before predicted her immediate demise, as the result of her imprudence. Who will say but what the exhalation from her numerous plants increasing the humidity of the atmosphere in which she lived, prolonged her life? The above is but one of many cases, in which tubercular consumption has been arrested and sometimes wholly cured by the sanitary effects produced by working among plants for a considerable time. We know of cases in which druggists, ministers, and students from school, compelled to relinquish their chosen vocations on account of failing health, have resorted to the nursery or hot-house. In almost every case restoration to vigorous health was the result.

We contend, therefore, that this old superstition that house plants are injurious to health, is nothing but a myth. The amount of carbonic acid gas at night discharged from two dozen large plants, will not equal that exhaled by one infant sleeper, as has been demonstrated by scientific men. Because a few old cronies stick to the absurdity that "plants are awful sickenin' things," it is no reason why sensible people should be at all alarmed by it.

CHAPTER X.

LAYERING.

Layering is a simple method by which plants may be multiplied. Moss Roses, nearly all kinds of hardy vines, like the Wistaria, Clematis, Honeysuckle, Ivy, and many others, are easily multiplied in this manner, together with most of our hardy shrubs. Many of our tenderer plants like Chrysanthemums, Verbenas, Heliotropes, etc., layer finely, by first bending the branches down to the ground, and partially covering them with sand or soil. Pots may be plunged in the ground so that the limbs will not require to be bent much in layering them. In layering hard-wooded plants like the Rose or Clematis, it is customary to cut a slight gash on the underside of each limb to be laid down, just cutting inside of the bark; this will arrest the flow of sap, and new roots will form at this point. Where vines are layered, such as the Grape, a simple twisting of the vine until the bark is cracked, will answer in place of cutting, and we believe it is just as well. It should be understood, however, that in layering, the entire shoot is not to be covered; a good portion of the tip of the shoot should be in sight, and only the middle of the branch be under ground, and securely fastened down by means of a peg. All layering should be done while the wood is young; just ripe enough to bend without snapping off, and all hardy vines and shrubs are in condition to layer from the first to the middle of June. For tender plants any month during the summer will answer for the operation. Most tender plants will root in a month or six weeks. Examine the layers in the fall, and if rooted, remove them; if not, they should remain undisturbed for another season.

CHAPTER XI.

PROPAGATION OF PLANTS FROM CUTTINGS.

In the propagation of plants from cuttings or otherwise, the amateur, with limited facilities, of course cannot compete with the trained and experienced propagator, who makes the rearing of plants his business, devoting his whole attention to that special branch. Many men have devoted the greater part of a lifetime to experiment and study, as to the best and most practicable methods for the successful propagation of plants. There are, however, common and ordinary methods for propagating plants from cuttings, that the most inexperienced can practice with a measure of success. All florists root their cuttings in sand, and that obtained from the beach of some fresh water lake is the best for the purpose, being free from gravel and clay, and will not hold water long. If lake sand cannot be easily obtained, common building sand will answer by thoroughly washing it with several waters to free it from clay, etc. I can recommend to the reader no more simple and practical method of propagating plants on a small scale, than the following, from the pen of an experienced florist, which expresses my own views exactly:

"Take a pan, or dish, at least three inches deep—the circumference of which may be as large as you wish, fill to within one half inch of the top with sand. The cuttings are to be inserted in the sand, which is made very wet, of the consistency of mud. The pan should then be placed on the window case, where it will receive the full light of the sun, which will not injure the cuttings in the least, providing the sand is kept constantly wet, being careful to never allow it to become dry for a moment, otherwise the plants will be lost.

"'Is there no drainage from the pan necessary?' none, the atmosphere will evaporate the water fast enough to prevent any stagnation during the brief time required for the cuttings to take root."

Success in propagating in this way, depends altogether upon keeping the sand wet like mud until the cuttings in it are "struck" or rooted, and this may be easily determined—with the hand gently try to lift the cutting, you will know if it is rooted by the hold maintained on the sand, if not, it will come out. A little experience in feeling with the hand in this way, will enable you to readily determine whether the cutting is rooted or not.

I have no doubt that the following table, which I have carefully prepared from my own extensive experience in regard to length of time required by different plants to take root from cuttings, will be of interest to all who desire to propagate plants in this manner. I am supposing now, in the following table, that all the conditions and facilities are such as are generally found in a first-class propagating house, with bottom heat, etc.:

	Days.
Ageratums	6 to 8
Amaranthus	6 " 8
Alyssum	10 " 12
Abutilon	12 " 15
Azalea	60 " 90
Begonias	12 " 15

Bouvardias	20 "	30
Clematis	30 "	40
Carnations	20 "	30
Cuphea (cigar plant)	6 "	8
Chrysanthemums	12 "	15
Centaurea	30 "	40
Coleus (all kinds)	6 "	8
Dahlias	15 "	20
Eupatoriums	15 "	20
Echeverias	30 "	40
Geraniums	12 "	15
Hibiscus	20 "	30
Heliotrope	12 "	15
Lobelia	12 "	15
Lantanas	12 "	15
Lavender	20 "	30
Mignonette	15 "	20
Myosotis	12 "	20
Nasturtium	10 "	12
Primroses	30 "	40
Pyrethrums	15 "	20
Poinsettia	30 "	40
Petunias	20 "	30
Roses	30 "	40
Oleander	30 "	40
Verbenas	6 "	8
Vinca	12 "	15

All hardy shrubs, taken when the wood is green and young, may be propagated in like manner. The summer is the time to take off the wood for such cuttings.

CHAPTER XII.

GRAFTING.

Grafting is a simple art, that both old and young should become acquainted with and be able to perform. In my garden there had stood, for a number of years, away in a corner by itself, a wild apple tree, which had sprung up from the seed; it always bore fruit, but of a worthless character, so sour and insipid that even the swine refused to devour it when it was thrown to them. I became tired of seeing this tree, and resolved to change its nature. I went to work, being a nurseryman, and procured cions of ten or a dozen different sorts of apple trees, and took the first favorable opportunity in the spring to graft my old and useless apple tree. When I had finished grafting, I found that I had inserted here and there on the different branches, fifty cions, all of which, with the exception of three, lived, grew, bore fruit, each "after its own kind," Baldwins, Greenings, Gravensteins, Spitzenbergs, etc., and it is now the most desirable tree in the garden; I completely transformed the nature of the tree. Any one who understands grafting can do the same thing. Apple, Pear, Plum, and Cherry trees can be successfully top-grafted in the manner spoken of above, and the month of April is the best time to perform the operation. The outfit necessary to perform the operation of grafting is a small hand-saw, a hatchet, a wedge, grafting-knife, and wax to cover the wound.

If the tree be a large one, and you wish to change the sort entirely, begin by sawing off all those limbs that, being removed, will leave enough to graft upon, and not spoil the symmetry of the tree. With the hand-saw saw off the limbs to be grafted about midway, then with the hatchet or wedge, cleave an opening in the remaining end of the limb, and entirely across, and deep enough to receive the cion; insert an iron in the cut to hold it open until the cion is placed, then withdraw the iron, and the graft will be held fast.

The cions to be inserted should be cut before ascending the tree to graft, and, together with the wax, can be carried in a small basket for the purpose. If the diameter of the limb to be grafted is more than an inch, it is best to insert two grafts, placed so that each cion will stand near the edge of the cut, in juxtaposition with the bark of the limb. Immediately after setting the graft, plaster the cut over with a heavy coat of wax, being careful to leave no crack or crevice open through which it would be possible for air or water to enter. Each cion, in wedge-grafting, is cut in the shape of a wedge; the whole cion need not be over three to four inches in length. The following is a good receipe for making grafting-wax: One and a half pound of bees-wax, six pounds of resin, and one and a half pound rough beef tallow; put all into a pot, and boil one half hour, keeping it stirred; pour it out into a tub of cold water, and when it is sufficiently stiff it should be gathered into balls. When wanted for use the balls should be laid in warm water, which will readily soften the wax; work the wax with the hands thoroughly before using. Wedge-grafting is by no means the only way to graft, although it is about the only method of grafting large trees. There are from ten to twenty other modes of grafting, the difference being in the manner of cutting the cion, and in fitting it to the stock. To go into detail in regard to them would occupy too much space in these limited pages. Any one, with a little practice, can learn to cut a cion, and to graft with success.

CHAPTER XIII.

HANGING BASKETS.—WARDIAN CASES AND JARDINIERES.

Hanging Baskets for plants are made of different materials, and in a great variety of forms. Some are made of wire, others of clay, and ornamented with fancy mouldings, etc. Very pretty baskets in rustic style are made by covering the outside of a wooden bowl with fantastic knots and roots; this makes a pleasing basket, but we know of none so desirable as the old style semi-globular wire basket, when properly filled.

DIRECTIONS FOR FILLING HANGING BASKETS.

To fill a wire basket, first obtain some of the green moss to be found on the lower portion of the trunks of trees in almost any shady piece of woods. This is to be used as a lining to the basket, turning the green side out, and entirely covering the inside of the wire form with the moss. Before filling the basket with soil, place a handful of charcoal or gravel in the bottom, which will hold the moisture. Fill the basket with rich, loose loam, such as will not harden by frequent waterings.

Plants that are peculiarly suitable for hanging baskets are quite numerous, and from them a selection may be made that will please the most exacting taste.

It is a mistake to crowd too many plants into a basket, if they grow they will soon become root-bound, stunted, and look sickly. If the hanging basket be of the ordinary size, one large and choice plant placed in the centre with a few graceful vines to droop over the edges, will have a better effect when established and growing, than if it were crowded with plants at the time of filling. Hanging baskets being constantly suspended, they are exposed to draughts of air from all sides, and the soil is soon dried out, hence careful watching is necessary in order to prevent the contents from becoming too dry. If the moss appears to be dry, take the basket down and dip it once or twice in a pail of water, this is better than sprinkling from a watering-pot. In filling hanging baskets, or vases of any kind, we invariably cover the surface of the soil with the same green moss used for lining, which, while it adds materially to the pleasing appearance of the whole, at the same time prevents the soil from drying out or becoming baked on the surface.

The following is a list of choice plants suitable for hanging-baskets. Those marked thus (+) are fine for the centre, those marked thus (*) have handsome foliage, and this mark (**) indicates that the plants have flowers in addition to handsome foliage:

- ** Begonia glaucophylla scandens.
- + Oxalis.
- ** Begonia Rex, very fine.
- * Fittonia
- + Cuphea platycentra (Cigar Plant).
- + Pandanus (Screw Pine).
- + Dracæna (Young's).
- + Neirembergia.
- + Centaurea gymnocarpa.
- ** Geraniums, Mrs. Pollock and Happy Thought.
- * Tradescantia discolor.
- * Peperomias.
- ** Gloxinias.
- * Fancy Ferns.
- + Ageratum (John Douglass, blue).
- + Achyranthes.
- ** Variegated Hydrangea.
- * Ficus Parcelli.
- ** Gesnerias.

* Variegated Grasses, etc., etc.

TRAILING PLANTS.

** Fuchsia, microphylla.
Sedum (Stone Crop).
** Ivy-leaved Geraniums.
German Ivy.
Indian Strawberry Vine.
Kenilworth Ivy.
Lycopodium.
Moneywort.
** Trailing Blue Lobelia.
* Cissus discolor.
** Lysimachia (Moneywort).
** Tropæolums.
** Torrenia Asiatica.
** Mesembryanthemums (Ice Plant).
** Cobæa scandens.
** Pilogyne suavis.
+ Lygodium scandens (Climbing Fern).

WARDIAN CASES—JARDINIERES, ETC.

A Wardian Case consists of a base, which is generally an oblong box, covered with a square glass frame, under which certain plants can be successfully grown. This is now considered by many to be a desirable ornament in the window-garden during the winter months. When neatly and artistically filled with suitable plants, a Wardian Case becomes a thing of beauty. These cases can be easily and cheaply made by any one possessed of ordinary mechanical skill. The base or box should be oblong in shape, at least eight inches deep, and lined inside with zinc or tin-plate, securely soldered to prevent the water and soil from staining the wood. A case made in this manner will endure a number of years without decaying. Over the case a square glass frame should be made to fit snugly; it should be from eighteen inches to two feet high, so as to allow the plants that are to grow under it plenty of room. When the case and frame are finished, the whole should be mounted upon a stand, or legs can be made with the case, under which are casters, by which to move it about easily. Before planting, make a small funnel hole through the bottom of the box, to allow the surplus water to escape rapidly, and before putting in the soil, cover the bottom of the box two inches deep with broken crocks or charcoal, or even gravel, to facilitate a rapid drainage, a matter absolutely essential to the healthy growth of the plants. Fill the box within an inch of the top with fine, rich, peaty loam, and all will be ready to receive the plants. Those suitable for growing in a case of this kind, should be such as will live and thrive in a moist, still atmosphere, and are of slow growth; all rampant, rank-growers must be discarded as being wholly unsuitable, as they would soon become of such proportions that they could not be confined in so limited a space. The following plants are eminently suited for Wardian Cases, Jardinieres, etc.; Fittonias (Gymnostachyum), Fancy Caladiums, Tradescantias, Cissus discolor, Gesnerias, some varieties of Crotons, Dwarf-growing Begonias, Fancy Ferns, Lycopods, etc., etc., are very suitable for this purpose. In arranging the plants in the case, particular care should be taken to have them so placed that the tallest-growing ones will be in the centre, and grading downward, according to size, the Lycopods being on the bottom. The whole surface of the soil may be covered with the trailing Lycopodium; by placing small pieces here and there, it will soon spread over the entire surface, making a beautiful ground work of purplish-green. Small, highly-colored sea-shells, and beautifully-colored pebbles, are scattered about among the plants, to enhance the beauty of the whole. After the case has been filled the soil should be thoroughly soaked with lukewarm water. Remove the case to a shady place for three or four days, to allow the plants to recuperate, after which it can be placed in the full light with safety. The lid or top should be lifted whenever there is excessive moisture on the inside, which will be indicated by the moisture trickling down on the inside of the glass. As a rule the plants should have fresh air, by lifting the lid for a few minutes each day, but beware of all cold draughts, or too much exposure to chilly atmospheres. Ordinarily, once a month is often enough to water, this must be governed by the circumstances, but they should never be allowed to become dry, remembering that as warmth, moisture, and a still atmosphere are secured, success will be certain.

CHAPTER XIV.

AQUATICS—WATER LILIES.

The native Water Lilies that abound in many of our lakes, ponds, and rivers, are more or less familiar to all. They grow up year after year through the placid waters, unfolding their blossoms of spotless purity to the silent stars, and after a short while, disappear, to return at another favorable season. The American Water Lily, *Nymphæa odorata*, has flowers of a yellowish-white, and an odor that is peculiar and pleasant. The size of the flowers averages three to four inches across. This is by no means the only aquatic lily, for we have in cultivation quite a number of other choice and striking species quite different in leaf and flower from *N. odorata*. Among the most noticeable of these is, *N. rubra*, a native of India, which has flowers of a rosy-red, measuring from eight to ten inches in diameter, with scarlet stamens; the large leaves of this Water Lily turn to a gorgeous crimson color in the fall. There are also *N. Devonensis*, bearing flowers of a brilliant red, which often measure from twelve to fourteen inches across, are star-shaped, and very beautiful. *N. cærulea*, a native of Egypt, has light blue flowers, and light green leaves; the flowers are very fragrant. *N. flava* has yellowish flowers, sometimes beautifully variegated with brown. There is quite a number of other interesting species, but those already mentioned are the best. The cultivation of Water Lilies is very simple, they can be grown with success in tubs or tanks, or in little artificial ponds, constructed to accommodate them. A hogshead sunk in the ground in the open air, in some sunny location, will answer to grow them in. Fill a hogshead half full of the compost recommended for aquatics, then set the plants in the compost, press down firmly, and fill the cask with pure water. If possible connect a flow and waste pipe with the barrel, to keep the water fresh, as this is highly essential in growing these plants in this manner.

A Mr. Sturtevant, we believe, now of Burlington Co., N. J., is an enthusiast on the cultivation of Water Lilies, and no doubt an excellent authority, He has written some valuable hints on the culture of aquatics, from which we are tempted to quote. He says, "I will add here a few words on the possibilities of aquatic gardening. One argument in favor of cultivating tropical lilies in the open air is, that larger leaves and flowers are obtained, and in case of the colored kinds, greater depth of color than when under glass." And again, "Let us suppose that you wish to have an aquatic garden, fifty, sixty, or a hundred feet in diameter. We will not build it in the stiff form of a circle or oval. There is a small bay, across which we will throw a rustic bridge to a peninsula: somewhere on the margin we will build a rustic summer-house."

"Now let us suppose that all has been planted, and come to mid-summer perfection. Some morning, before the night-blooming lilies (there are varieties that bloom only in the night), have taken their mid-day sleep, let us ascend the tower, and take a view of the picture." He graphically describes the beauty of this miniature Eden, with all its rare and beautiful tropical plants, which certainly must be enchanting for any who love the beautiful. It is surprising that many people of ample means, and with good facilities for growing aquatics, and who have a taste for flowers, do not take more interest in domesticating these plants. Any one who keeps a gardener can have a very fine show of these beautiful flowers, and a comparatively small outlay will bring good results in a short time. Let those who can, try it.

SOIL FOR GROWING AQUATIC PLANTS.

The best soil for growing aquatics, is that obtained from the bed of a pond, or a slow, swampy stream, but when this is not readily obtainable, a mixture of equal parts of good, rich garden loam and stable manure will be almost as good. Some use a mixture of muck and bog peat, from which they claim very satisfactory results in growing aquatics; either we think can be used with good success.

CHAPTER XV.

HARDY CLIMBING VINES.—IVIES.

Hardy Climbing Vines seem to be in large demand in different sections of the country, either for training upon trellises as single specimens, or for training upon the side of the building, piazza, portico, or to screen unsightly places, etc. We select from a large number of hardy climbing vines the following sorts, which we think are the most desirable:

- Wistaria, Chinese (blue and white).
- Honeysuckles, Belgian.
- Clematis Jackman's (purple).
- Clematis Henry's (pure white).
- Clematis, *viticella rubra grandiflora* (red).
- Virginia Creeper, *Ampelopsis quinquefolia* (strong grower).
- Japan Creeper, *Ampelopsis tricuspidata*, or *Veitchii*, of most catalogues.
- Bignonia, Trumpet-Flower.
- Rose, Baltimore Belle (white).
- Rose, Queen of the Prairies (pink).

All of the above named vines are strong, vigorous growers, perfectly hardy, and with the exception of the two Creepers, are handsome bloomers.

IVIES—GROWING AND TRAINING.

> "A dainty plant is the Ivy green,
> That creepeth o'er ruins old."—Boz.

The Ivy is one of the oldest and most venerable of all climbing shrubs, and is preëminently the poet's vine. In some of the older countries, especially in England, where the climate is particularly favorable to its growth, the Ivy is very attractive, and is said to reach the greatest perfection there. Travellers who have journeyed through that country, describe the old Ivy as clinging closely to, and completely covering the walls of ancient castles, and churches, and often it runs rampant over the fields, mounting stone walls, clinging to trees, etc. The Ivy in our climate is entirely hardy, enduring the severest winters without any protection. If the vine is allowed to grow over the walls of a dwelling, either on the inside, in a living-room, or on the outer walls of the building, is not only beautiful as an ornament of the home, but beneficial; in a sanitary point of view it is regarded as useful. Some plants of Ivy growing in the living and sleeping rooms, will do more to keep the atmosphere of the apartments pure and wholesome, than anything we can possibly imagine, and I recommend their more extensive cultivation in malarial localities. The Ivy may be easily cultivated from slips or layers. In soil, sand, or even in pure water, cuttings will root, and they will take up with almost any kind of soil, but that which can be easily kept loose, is preferable. The Ivy is partial to shade, and if it never saw the sun it would make no difference, as it would grow and flourish just the same. There is no sight more attractive in a window-garden than a fine Ivy vine trained up the casement, over the wall and ceiling; its dark, rich, glossy leaves, and thrifty look, make it an object to be admired. If grown in pots in the house, the soil will soon become exhausted, if the plant is growing rapidly, and it should be changed or enriched with decayed manure at least once each year, care being taken not to disturb the roots to a great extent. It is a mistake to allow Ivies too much pot-room, they will do better if the roots are considerably confined. Soap-suds or liquid manure if applied once a mouth when the plants are growing, will promote a luxuriant growth. When dust accumulates on the leaves, as it will, if grown in-doors, wash it off with a damp cloth or sponge; if this is long neglected, you need not be surprised if you soon discover the leaves to be covered with red-spider or scale-lice. Cold water is the best wash, when washing be sure and treat the underside of the leaves as well as the upper surface. I would recommend the "English Ivy" as being the best sort for general cultivation.

CHAPTER XVI.

ANNUAL FLOWERING PLANTS.—PANSY CULTURE.

Annuals flower the same season the seeds are sown, perfect their seeds, and then die. "There is," says James Vick, "No forgotten spot in the garden, none which early flowering bulbs or other spring flowers have left unoccupied, that need remain bare during the summer. No bed but what can be made brilliant with these favorites, for there is no situation or soil in which some of these favorites will not flourish. Some delight in shade, others in sunshine; some are pleased with a cool, clay bed, while others are never so comfortable as in a sandy soil, or burning sun. The seed, too, is so cheap as to be within the reach of all, while a good collection of bedding plants would not come within the resources of many, and yet very few beds filled with expensive bedding plants look as well as a good bed of our best annuals, like Phlox, Petunia, or Portulaca, and for a vase or basket many of our annuals are unsurpassed. To annuals, also, we are indebted mainly for our brightest and best flowers in the late summer and autumn months.

"Without the Phlox and Petunia, and Portulaca and Aster, and Stock, our autumn gardens would be poor indeed, and how we would miss the sweet fragrance of the Alyssum, Mignonette, and Sweet Pea, if any ill-luck should befall them, or deprive us of these sweet favorites!" Annuals are divided into three classes, hardy, half-hardy, and tender. The hardy annuals are those that, like the Larkspur, Candytuft, etc., may be sown in the autumn, or very early in the spring in the open ground. The half-hardy annuals should not be sown in the open ground until all danger of frost is over. The Balsams and Marigolds belong to this class. The tender annuals generally require starting in a green-house, or hot-bed, to bring them to perfection, and should not be set in the open ground until the weather is fine and warm, some time in June. From a perplexing number to be found in plant catalogues, we select the following twelve sorts of annuals as being the most desirable for the garden; they are a galaxy of gems, indeed:

- Asters,

- Balsams,
- Phlox Drummondii,
- Double Petunias,
- Pansies,
- Double Sweet Alyssum,
- Double White Pyrethrum,
- Dwarf Ageratum,
- Verbenas,
- Salvias,
- Double Stocks,
- Celosias (Coxcomb).

Sow the seed in the open ground the latter part of May, and the first of July most of the sorts will be in bloom, and they will continue to bloom until arrested by frosts.

PANSY CULTURE.

Pansies are old and popular favorites, they embrace varieties with variously-colored flowers, from almost jet black, to pure white and yellow. They are easily grown from seed. The general custom is to sow Pansy seed in the fall, but we are in favor of spring sowing. We have tried sowing seed at both seasons, and find that plants grown from spring-sown seed bloom more freely throughout the hot months of summer, while plants raised by fall sowing become exhausted, and cease flowering much sooner. Seed sown in March, in light, rich soil, will make fine blooming plants the same season. Pansies are hardy, if they have good protection with a litter of leaves or straw, or any light covering, which should be removed very early in the spring, or as soon as danger of heavy frosts is over. Plants remaining in ground through the winter, if proper care is given them, will bloom very early in the spring, as soon as the frost is out of the ground. We have even seen the frail blossoms peeping up through the snow, but the plants become exhausted and cease flowering before mid-summer. It is possible to have them bloom throughout the entire winter by taking up old plants from the open ground in October, and carefully planting them in a tight, cold frame in a sheltered location, covering the frame with glazed sash. This is often done by florists whose trade demands the flowers at that season of the year, and especially early in spring. Treated thus, they flower abundantly. The same can be done with Violets. Pansies require a partial shade and a good, rich, loamy soil, and an occasional watering through the dry season will help them.

CHAPTER XVII.

FALL OR HOLLAND BULBS.

That class of bulbs known as Fall, or Holland Bulbs, includes Hyacinths, Crocuses, Jonquils, Tulips, Narcissuses, Snow-drops, and several less known kinds. These bulbs are grown in Holland in immense quantities, the soil and climate of that country being peculiarly favorable to them, and they are annually imported into this country in great numbers. The fall is the time to set them out; any time from the first of October, to the middle of December. Tulips, Jonquils, Narcissuses, and Hyacinths, should be planted four inches deep, and eight inches apart each way; the Snow-drops and Crocuses two inches deep, and six inches apart.

All of the above named bulbs are entirely hardy, and will stand in the ground without any surface protection through the severest winters. Some go to the trouble of covering the surface with leaves or other litter for protection, but this is entirely unnecessary. A very pretty effect may be had, where one has a large number of bulbs, by selecting the different colors and planting each color in a row by itself, so that when they blossom, it will be in ribbon-lines of red, white, blue, or yellow, as the case may be. Or, if one has a large number of beds of different shapes, cut so as to form a design of some kind, each section may be planted with a different color (Hyacinths are the best for this work), and when all come into bloom in April, the effect will be most charming. We tried this "massing" of the differently colored bulbs one year, in a "design" of one hundred different sections of all conceivable shapes. Planting the bulbs so that, when in blossom, the whole would present a harmonious effect. It would be hard to conceive of a more attractive sight than that presented by all those bulbs in full bloom in early April, when every thing else looked barren and cheerless. They were admired by every one who saw them. Bulbs of this character bloom and pass away in season to allow room for other plants to be set out. These may be set between the rows of bulbs, and not disturb them in the least. Any of the above named bulbs are especially desirable for house culture in winter. Make an oblong box, say four feet in length, fifteen inches wide, and twelve deep, fill this with fine, rich loam, then plant a row of Hyacinths in the centre, and on each side of this plant a row of either Snow-drops or Crocuses, water thoroughly, and set away in a dark, cool place. In three weeks remove the box into the full light, and water freely, they will grow and bloom throughout the winter. If the box can be set near a front window, it will make a pretty display while the bulbs are in bloom.

These bulbs can be started in pots, or glasses filled with water, and treated in the same manner as stated above. Place a single bulb of Hyacinth in each pot or glass. Four-inch pots filled nearly to the top with soil, and the bulbs set in and pressed down, so that nothing but the crown is above ground, are all that is necessary. The same bulbs can be used a number of years, but they are not so good as fresh ones, which should be obtained each year if possible. After the bulbs are through blooming, they may be left in the soil in which they grew through the winter, and removed to a dry place to rest, in preparation for starting them another fall. If fresh bulbs are desired for this purpose, the old ones may be planted out in the open ground, where they will again renew their strength, and bloom annually for a number of years. They are multiplied from the seed and from offshoots.

CHAPTER XVIII.

TROPICAL BULBS.—TUBEROSES.

Gladioluses, Tuberoses, Cannas, and Caladiums, come under this head, and are the best known of this class of bulbs. They are not hardy, and the slightest frost will injure them more or less. It is customary to allow tender bulbs of this kind to rest during the winter, the same as one would an onion. They can be safely kept through the winter under the staging of the greenhouse, in a dry, frost-proof cellar, where there is plenty of light, or in any other place where potatoes can be safely stored. Tropical bulbs of all kinds are much benefited by planting them in good, light, loamy soil, well enriched with well-rotted stable manure. They may be planted out in the open ground as soon as it can be worked in the spring, and all danger from heavy frosts is over. Any of the above named bulbs of ordinary size, should be planted at least from three to four inches deep, and from six to eight inches deep when the bulbs are of extra size. I am in favor of planting these bulbs in the open ground much earlier than most gardeners are in the habit of doing. Experience has shown me that the earlier in spring those summer bulbs are set out in the open ground, the better. Just as soon as the ground is in good condition to work, spade it up deeply, and plant the bulbs; the roots will soon begin to develop in the cool ground, before the tops start to grow, which is the true principle in growing all plants. They will thus receive a fine start before hot weather sets in. We have had Tuberoses and Gladioluses to bloom much earlier than usual, and much more continuously throughout the summer and fall, as the result of planting them as soon as the ground can be worked in the spring. If a continuation of bloom is desired, the bulbs should be planted at successive intervals of not less then three weeks; this will give a sucession of bloom throughout the entire season. In the fall remove the bulbs from the ground as soon as the tops have been touched by frost, cutting the stalk off to within a couple of inches of the base, and setting the bulbs away to rest for the winter.

TUBEROSES.

No collection of garden flowers is complete without the Tuberose. For the spotless purity of its flowers, and for incomparable fragrance, it has no superior. It is very easy to grow them successfully. Bulbs intended for fall blooming, should be planted in the open ground from the first to the middle of May; plant them about two inches deep. They will do well in any good, rich garden soil, if the soil is occasionally moved around them with the rake or hoe, after they are up and growing. Such treatment will cause the bulbs to grow rapidly, and the flower trusses, when they come into bloom, will consequently be much larger and finer. As the Tuberose is not hardy in our Northern climates, the bulbs should be dug up in the fall, the tops or stalks removed to within two or three inches of the bulbs, which should then be laid away in some dry, warm place, a dry and frost-proof cellar will do, or better yet, store them if possible, under the staging of a green-house. In the spring, before planting, remove all the young offsets from around the parent bulb; there are usually a number of young shoots clinging to it, and as the old bulb blooms but once, and only once, it is henceforth good for nothing, save for the production of more bulbs, if desired.

The young offshoots of the first season's growth will not become blooming bulbs until the third year, but if you have quite a number of young bulbs, say twenty-five or fifty, there will naturally be a number that will bloom in rotation, from year to year, and give some bloom each season. Some enterprising florists have Tuberoses nearly the whole year round. In order to do this, the bulbs must be "started" in pots; the bulbs are potted in the usual manner, so that the top, or crown of the bulb, when potted, will just show above the soil, and they should be kept rather dry until they show signs of growing, when they can be watered freely and set in a warm place. Of course bulbs intended for winter blooming must rest, or be kept from growing during the summer, and bulbs to be in bloom in April or May, must be started in January or February in pots. Tuberoses are rapidly productive; ten old bulbs having been known to produce one hundred young offshoots in one season. There are many "fine points" in growing Tuberoses, but the instruction here given will enable any one to grow them successfully.

CHAPTER XIX.

ROSES—CULTIVATION AND PROPAGATING.

The Rose is preëminently the Queen of Flowers. It has no rival in the floral kingdom, and will always stand at the head in the catalogue of Flora's choicest gems. To it alone belongs that subtle perfume that captivates the sense of smell, and that beauty of form and color so pleasing to the eye. Add to all this, it is one of the easiest plants to cultivate, as it will grow and flower in almost any soil or climate, requiring but little care and attention as compared with many other favorites of the garden. There has been great improvement made in Roses in the last twenty years by skillful cultivators in this country and in Europe, and from a few common sorts formerly grown, many hundred choice and desirable varieties have been produced, and to-day the choice cultivated varieties are very numerous. These differ in respect to hardiness, habit of growth, and peculiar characteristics of blooming, and for these reasons cultivators have grouped them into several distinct classes, each class differing in certain characteristics from the others.

TEA ROSES.

The Roses best adapted for in-door culture belong to the class known as Tea Roses; these are tender, of a bushy growth, and if properly treated, will bloom the year round; the flowers have a strong tea-scent.

Tea Roses can be cultivated out-of-doors with success, but they must be taken up in the fall and removed in-doors. We know it is the custom of some gardeners to lay the bushes down in the fall, and cover them with earth and leaves; while in some cases this may preserve them, it cannot be depended on as a rule. To keep up a steady bloom, pinch off all flowers as soon as they begin to fade. It is best to not let the buds open fully while on the bush, but they should be cut in the bud, and placed in a vase of water, where they will expand and keep for a long while. All dead leaves and flower stems should be carefully removed, and the surface of the soil in the pots should be stirred up occasionally with a stick, this will keep the plants in a growing condition, and if they can be kept growing, they will bloom continuously.

The following varieties of Tea Roses are in every respect among the best for house culture:

Bon Silene.—Flowers purplish-carmine; highly scented.

Niphetos.—Pure white, magnificent long buds; an incessant bloomer.

Perle de Jardins.—Sulphur-yellow, full and double; a splendid rose.

La France (Bourbon).—Bright lilac-rose, fine form; perpetual bloomer, half hardy.

Hermosa (Bourbon).—Light rose-color, cupped-shaped; a most perpetual bloomer.

HYBRID PERPETUAL, AND MOSS ROSES.

Both of the above classes are entirely distinct from either the Tea, Noisette, or Bourbon Roses; they are entirely hardy, exceedingly free-bloomers in their season—from June to July; their flowers have a delightful perfume, and are noted for the richness and variety of their colors. They require to be closely pruned annually. The spring is the most desirable time to prune. They should have a top-dressing of manure every fall. The ground should be kept well shaded around their roots in summer. They require a strong, rich soil to make them flower well. These roses are not desirable for house culture. The following are among the best varieties of the Hybrid Perpetual, or Remontant Roses:

Gen. Jacqueminot.—Brilliant crimson-scarlet; magnificent buds.

La Reine.—Deep rosy-pink; an ideal rose.

Coquette des Alps.—White; blooms in clusters.

Black Prince.—Blackish-crimson; large, full, and globular.

Victor Verdier.—Rich deep-rose; elegant buds.

MOSS ROSES.

Of this class we need not speak in detail to any who have ever seen its delicate moss-covered buds, and inhaled their delightful odor. They are perfectly hardy, and can be wintered without any protection. They are called perpetual, but this is a misnomer, for we know but one variety of Moss Rose that approaches it, that is the *Salet* Moss. The rest are no more so than are the so-called Hybrid Perpetuals.

Moss Roses should be severely pruned in spring, removing all the old wood.

Salet, deep pink; *White Perpetual,* pure white; and *Crested,* rose-color, are the most desirable sorts.

PROPAGATING THE ROSE.

The Rose is somewhat difficult to propagate from cuttings, and it takes from three to four weeks for them to root under the best conditions. Moss Roses are generally multiplied by layering (see "Layering"), and by budding on the common Manetti or Multiflora stocks. The following will be found to be a very practicable and simple method of propagating roses on a small scale, and is attended with very little trouble or expense: In the fall place sand in a box, or cold frame, to the depth of eight inches. Take from the bushes the number of cuttings it is desired to propagate, making them with two or three points or eyes; insert them in the sand (which should be previously packed as solid as can be), then water thoroughly. As the cuttings are to remain in this frame all winter, it should be provided with a glass sash, and the whole covered with leaves and manure. It need not be banked up until freezing weather. If rightly done, we may expect at the least fifty per cent of the cuttings to come from their winter bed finely rooted. They should then be potted, and after growing awhile, planted out, and some of them will bloom the first season.

CHAPTER XX.

JAPAN AND OTHER LILIES.—CALLA LILIES.

If we call the rose the "Queen of Flowers," what royal title shall we bestow upon the beautiful Japan Lilies? We sometimes think it would be proper to name the Rose the King, for its commanding aspect, and the grandly beautiful Lily, the Queen of the floral kingdom. But, be this as it may, we have only to gaze upon a collection of Japan Lilies when in full bloom, and inhale their delicious odor, that perfumes the whole atmosphere, to be convinced of their superiority over all other flowers. Surely Solomon in all his glory was not arrayed like one of these.

There are many different species and varieties of Lilies, but none approach those known as Japan Lilies in the beauty and variety of their flowers, and their exquisite fragrance. They are perfectly hardy, and the fall is the proper time to plant them. If good strong bulbs are set out in the ground in October or November, planted about eight inches deep, they will throw up strong shoots the following summer, and bloom freely. The flowers increase in size and beauty with the age of the bulb, and this should be left to grow undisturbed in the same spot for five or six years; afterwards, if desired, the bulbs can be dug up, the offshoots removed, and the old bulbs reset, and they will do better than ever. Any of the young bulbs that have been removed can be planted out in the ground, and in a few years will form good blooming bulbs. The time to perform this work is in the fall. Although entirely hardy without protection, it will benefit these lilies very much, if during the winter, they are covered with a coarse litter, leaves or any other good covering. This should be raked off early in the spring, as manure of any kind seems to injure them when they come in contact with it. The soil in which they do best is a light, sandy loam, well drained. The lily flourishes best in sunny locations. The following is a description of the leading varieties:

LILIUM AURATUM.—This is the well-known Gold-banded Lily, and most decidedly the finest of all the Japan Lilies.

L. CANDIDUM.—The old White Lily (not Japan) of the gardens; a splendid sort; elegant, large, pure white flowers, in clusters; blooms earlier than the others, but not the first year; it is one of the most beautiful Lilies.

L. CITRINUM.—Very rare and beautiful; large, elegantly formed flowers; color, pale yellow, exquisitely tinged with blush.

L. LONGIFLORUM.—Exceedingly beautiful; very long trumpet-shaped flowers, pure snow white.

L. SPECIOSUM RUBRUM.—One of the finest of Japan Lilies; bright crimson and white spotted; splendid large flower, borne in clusters, stem two to three feet.

L. TIGRINUM—SINGLE TIGER LILY.—This splendid Lily is one of the best in the list; the stem is tall; the flowers large and elegantly formed; blooms in large clusters; color, brilliant orange scarlet with intense black spots; remains in bloom a long time.

L. UMBELATUM.—Very showy, brilliant red, variegated flowers in clusters.

THE CALLA LILY.

The Calla Lily, or "The Lily of the Nile," is an old and popular favorite, and is found in window-garden collections everywhere. It is a native of the tropics, where it is said it grows to an enormous size; a single flower often measuring one to two feet in diameter. The Calla will attain its highest perfection if planted in a rich, mucky soil, obtained from a swamp or bog. It also requires an abundance of water during the growing season. Callas, like all other bulbous plants, must have a season of rest. If required to bloom during the winter or spring months, they must be rested in the summer season, if this is not done we must not expect to have any success in flowering them. The blooming season can be reversed if desired, by resting in winter. Without allowing them at least three months of rest, it is useless to expect to flower them successfully. By "resting," we mean to withhold water, and allow the leaves and stalks to die down completely to the bulb. Then turn the pot on its side under a tree or grape-arbor, and let the soil dry up completely; this will kill the stalk but not injure the bulb.

HOW TO PREPARE CALLAS FOR WINTER BLOOMING.

After three months of this rest; or about the first of October, we "dump" out the plant, shake off all the old soil from the bulb or bulbs, and re-pot in fine, rich soil, using pots one size larger than those used the previous year; place the plants in a cool, shady spot, and water freely. Let them remain for two or three weeks, until new roots have formed, after which all danger is passed, and they can be removed into full light and heat. When growing, water freely. An application of strong liquid-manure once a week will add greatly to the growth of the plants, and to the number of blossoms produced. A very pretty effect can be obtained by arranging the plants about a fountain or pond where they will bloom freely throughout the summer season, presenting a tropical appearance. They will also grow well by standing the pots completely in the water.

CHAPTER XXI.

GERANIUMS—THE BEST TWELVE SORTS.

There is no flower that can surpass the Geranium for profusion of bloom, brilliancy and variety of color, and general adaptability for house culture. The following are the best twelve sorts:

DOUBLE VARIETIES.

Madam Ballet, pure white; Jewel, dark crimson; Asa Gray, salmon, very free bloomer; Madam Lemoine, light pink, large trusses; Bishop Wood, rich scarlet, approaching to carmine; Charmieux, scarlet; Casimer Perrier, a very near approach to yellow

SINGLE VARIETIES.

New Life, variegated, crimson, and white; Gen. Grant, dazzling scarlet; Pauline Lucca, pure white, with pink-eye; Chief Justice, the darkest of all Geraniums, immense trusses; Pinafore, salmon, with white eye; La Vienne, pure white, pale stamens, splendid; Master Christine, light pink, elegant for bedding.

CHAPTER XXII.

AZALEAS; HOW TO CULTIVATE THEM.

Comparatively few of these charming plants are to be seen outside of greenhouses and private conservatories, we know not for what reasons, unless it be the erroneous idea that they cannot be successfully grown unless one has the facilities of the florist. I think there is no class of plants more easy of culture, when the manner of treating them is once understood, than Azaleas. As they are decidedly winter-flowering plants, generally coming into bloom from December to March and April, they must be treated as such. They should have the same kind of treatment during the summer as recommended for Camellias, allowing them to rest in some cool, shady spot out-of-doors, during which period the flowering shoots will grow that are to give the bloom through the winter months. They can be taken into the house any time in the fall before freezing weather, and they will thrive well in an atmosphere suited to the generality of plants, although to bring the bloom out to the best, an atmosphere of 55° is needed.

There are over one hundred distinct varieties, ranging from pure white to lilac-purple, scarlet and pink, and when in full bloom the entire plant might be easily mistaken for a large bouquet, so literally covered is it with dazzling blossoms.

One or two varieties of Azaleas should grace every collection; almost every florist keeps them in stock, and the price asked is but a small consideration compared with the amount of pleasure one will derive by having them in full bloom himself.

Florists hardly ever attempt to multiply the Azaleas from cuttings, on account of the hardness of the wood, but the common mode of multiplying them is by grafting on the stock of the Wild Azalea, plants being easily and quickly obtained through this method. The Azalea will flourish best with a rich, mucky loam, a rather shady locality, and an abundance of water.

CHAPTER XXIII.

CAMELLIAS.—ORANGE AND LEMON TREES.

Dear reader, did you ever see a large Camellia plant in full blossom? If you have not, I will risk my reputation by saying that all other flowers within my knowledge, barring the rose, dwindle into insignificance when compared with it. It excels the finest rose in doubleness and form of its flowers, and puts the virgin lily to shame for spotless purity and whiteness; if it only possessed fragrance, it would be unquestionably the Queen of the floral world. What I shall have to say in regard to this plant, I hope will have the effect of introducing it into many homes where it has hitherto been little known. Few outside of professional florists have undertaken to cultivate the Camellia, for the reason, we suppose, that it is thought to be quite an impossibility to raise and bloom it successfully outside of a green-house; this is a mistake, although many believe it otherwise. I contend that Camellias can be as easily and as successfully grown in the window-garden as the Rose or Geranium.

Camellias bloom in the winter, and at no other season of the year. Plants should be purchased of the florist in the fall or early in winter, and such plants as have flower-buds already formed; those plants, if kept in the right atmosphere, will bloom profusely, but they must have an atmosphere of 50° until the buds are all expanded, after which there will be no danger of the flowers blasting. As soon as the bloom has all passed off, the plants should be taken from their cool quarters, and placed with the other plants in a warm temperature, and watered freely, to encourage a vigorous growth previous to removing them out-of-doors in the spring. As soon as all danger of heavy frosts is over in the spring, the plants should be taken from the house and removed to some shady location, under a grape-arbor, in a pit or frame covered with shades; here leave them standing in the pots "plunging" the pots in earth or sand to prevent too rapid drying out.

The summer is the period in which the flower-buds are formed that bloom in winter; the plants should be kept growing, and watered freely throughout the summer. They must be left out-of-doors as long as the weather will permit, but, on the approach of frost, take the plants into the house, and let them stand in a cool room, where the temperature is not over 50°. This is the critical time, for if they are removed into a warm temperature of 70° or 80°, the buds will all blast and drop off, and no flowers will be produced.

If the plants are large and well-budded, a succession of bloom will be yielded throughout the entire winter. There are a number of varieties, embracing colors from red, pink, variegated, etc., to the purest waxy-white. The Double White Camellia Japonica, the white sort, is the most valuable for its bloom, the flowers being sometimes four to five inches in diameter, exceedingly double, with the petals imbricated, and of a waxy texture, and are highly prized by florists, who often charge as high as one dollar per flower for them. They are invaluable for funeral occasions, when pure white flowers are required. Plants are multiplied by either grafting or budding them on the common stock; it is almost impossible to raise plants from cuttings; they are slower than the Azalea to take root.

ORANGE AND LEMON TREES.

Both Orange and Lemon trees can be easily raised by sowing the seeds in good, rich soil, and after the seedlings become of sufficient size, a foot to fifteen inches high, they should be budded or grafted, otherwise blossoms and fruit cannot be expected. In the tropical climes, where these fruits are grown, there are varieties that spring up from the seeds of sweet oranges, called naturals; these yield a fruit that is edible, but is of an insipid taste. In no case can we obtain edible fruit of either Oranges or Lemons, budded or unbudded, in northern climates. The best time to bud these trees is when the seedlings are about a year old. They can be budded in the same manner as other trees, and as a rule, the buds take readily if the stock is in the right condition. Some graft them, but buds take better than grafts, and grow more rapidly. If the budding is successful, and the bud looks fresh and green in two weeks after it has been inserted, the union has taken place. The stock may then be cut off within two inches of the bud, and after the bud has started to grow, cut the stub still lower down, close to the bud. One bud in each stock is better than three or four. The soil best adapted to these trees is a rich, mucky loam. They should have plenty of pot room when growing, and, if possible, a warm, moist atmosphere.

CHAPTER XXIV.

FUCHSIAS—TRAINING AND MANAGEMENT

We confess to have a special liking for the Fuchsias, and think no assortment of house plants is complete without one or two varieties of these beautiful flowers. They are easily propagated, either from cuttings or by layers, and the amount of bloom one strong, healthy plant is capable of producing under favorable circumstances, is truly wonderful. Upon one plant of Fuchsia speciosa, started from a cutting of a single eye in March, we counted at one time, in the December following, one hundred and fifty perfect blossoms. The plant stood in an eight-inch pot, and measured four feet in hight. Some kinds do better as house plants than others, among the best are *F. speciosa, F. fulgens,* and the Rose of Castile, and I would particularly recommend these sorts as superior to all others for the window-garden. The right kind of soil has everything to do with success in growing fine Fuchsias; it should be of a light peaty quality, with one-third cow manure, and thoroughly mixed together until well decayed. They also relish an abundance of water; and if they have, while growing, an application of liquid manure once or twice a week, it will be beneficial; never allow the roots to become potbound, but when the roots begin to form a mat on the outside of the ball of earth, it is time to shift the plant into a pot of the next larger size, and so on as the plant requires it. This is a very important point, and should not be overlooked if strong, healthy plants are expected.

Fuchsias are especially desirable for training on trellises. They can be trained over an upright trellis, and have a very pretty effect, but the best form is that of an umbrella. Secure a strong, vigorous plant, and allow one shoot to grow upright until about two feet high, then pinch off the top of the shoot. It will branch out and form a head, each shoot of which, when sufficiently long, may have a fine thread or hair-wire attached to the tip, by which to draw it downward; fasten the other end of the wire or thread to the stem of the plant, and all the shoots will then be pendent. When each of these branches has attained a length of eight inches, pinch off the tip, and the whole will form a dense head, resembling an umbrella in shape, and the graceful flowers pendent from each shoot will be handsome indeed. Remember to keep the stock clear of side-shoots, in order to throw the growth into the head.

If properly taken care of, most Fuchsias will bloom the year round, but some kinds can be especially recommended for winter blooming, among them are *F. speciosa*, flesh-colored, with scarlet corolla; *F. serratifolia*, orange-scarlet corolla, greenish sepals; Meteor, deep-red corolla, light-pink sepals. The following are the finest in every respect that the market affords: Mrs. Bennett, pink; Sir Cohn Campbell, double blue; Rose of Castile, single violet; Elm City, double scarlet; Carl Holt, crimson; Tower of London, double blue; Wave of Life, foliage yellow, corolla violet; *F. speciosa*, single, flesh-colored, and *F. fulgens*, long red corolla.

CHAPTER XXV.

CACTUSES.—NIGHT-BLOOMING CEREUS.—REX BEGONIAS.

For singularity and grotesqueness of form, as well as for the exceptional conditions under which they grow to the best advantage, no class of plants is more remarkable than the *Cactaceæ*. Of these, about a thousand species have been described by botanists; nearly all are indigenous to the New World, though but a small proportion are in cultivation. Cactuses delight in a dry, barren, sandy soil. They are naturally children of the desert. It is said by travellers that many of the species bear edible fruit, resembling somewhat in taste the gooseberry. So much for the peculiarities of the Cactus family in its native localities, but how can we succeed in cultivating the plants with satisfactory results in the window-garden?

There are two simple methods of treatment that Cactuses should receive, namely: First, keep the soil about them constantly dry, and keep them in a warm place. Secondly, the soil should be of a poor quality, mixed with a little brick dust, and they should never be allowed too much pot room. If either of these two points are observed in the treatment of Cactuses, there will be no difficulty in keeping them in a flourishing condition all the time.

THE NIGHT-BLOOMING CEREUS.

The Night-blooming Cereus is an interesting plant, and excites much admiration when in flower, as it blooms at night-time only, the flowers closing up when exposed to the day-light. They are magnificent flowers when in full blow, but, unhappily, are short-lived, a flower never opening a second time. The plant belongs to the Cactus Family, and requires the same general treatment. There are a number of night-flowering species and varieties, but the one especially known as the Night-blooming Cereus is *Cereus grandiflorus*, which, when in full bloom, presents a rare sight. Some of the flowers of the night-blooming kinds are exceedingly fragrant, notably

Cereus triangularis, a single flower of which, when in fall bloom, will fill the air of a room with its pleasant odor. These plants can be made to bloom freely by keeping the soil quite dry, and allowing them very little pot-room, as they depend more upon the atmosphere than the soil for their growth. We have known large plants of *Cereus grandiflorus*, to produce as many as twenty-five fine blossoms each in the course of a season. We have found that liquid manure, if applied to these plants about once a month, and when the soil about them is very dry, will work wonders in their growth, and when a rapid growth can be obtained, there will be no trouble in having an abundance of flowers at regular intervals. Care must be taken not to have the liquid too strong. A small quantity of brick dust, mixed with the soil in which they are growing, will be beneficial. These species of Cereus are easily propagated by cuttings, which will root readily in sand of any kind. Being of a slender habit of growth, and rather rampant, they should have some sort of support, and it is advisable to either train them to a trellis, or upon wires, or a string stretched over and along the window sash. We have had a number of flowers of a pure feathery white, *C. grandiflorus*, that were over fifteen inches in diameter; this is the best of the night-flowering species.

PROPAGATING REX BEGONIAS.

Those Begonias, known as belonging to the Rex division, are very beautiful, and also very distinct in both leaf and flower from all other species and varieties. The leaves are noted for their peculiar shape and markings, making them very valuable as ornamental house plants. They are easily multiplied from the leaf with its stalk. To propagate these, the leaf, or leaves, including the stalk, should be taken off close to the plant. Insert the stem of the leaf in sand, and deep enough to allow the leaf to lie flat upon the surface of the sand. It will take them about from two to three weeks to root, after which they should be potted in good, rich soil. It will take sometime to start them into a growth, but they grow very rapidly when they begin, and in two years will make large plants.

CHAPTER XXVI.

ROCKERIES—HOW TO MAKE THEM.

Many have a taste for forming grotesque pieces of rock work, selecting therefor such oddly-shaped and variously-colored rocks as may be gathered near the locality; these are generally piled in the form of a pyramid in a conspicuous place on the lawn, and if nicely arranged, cannot be surpassed in attractiveness, and are in pleasing contrast with the flower-beds and shrubbery. Some prefer to have merely the bare rocks heaped into a pile, which will appear grotesque and rugged; others set out suitable plants, and train vines to creep over them. We think the latter the best method, where common rocks are used, but if one is fortunate enough to live in a locality where a large number of variously-colored rocks can be obtained, their natural colors when arranged will make them highly attractive. One of the finest pieces of work of this kind we ever saw, was formed of a number of rocks gathered from almost every country on the globe, each stone having a peculiar tint of its own. On the top of this valuable pile was a rare specimen of Red Rock obtained from Siberia, in the region of eternal frost.

HOW TO MAKE A ROCKERY.

Having selected a site in a partly shaded spot, we will then proceed to form a mound of earth which may be drawn to the spot for the purpose if necessary. Upon and around this mound the rocks are to be placed, one layer thick, leaving here and there between them a small crevice in which to plant vines, or to drop a few seeds. The top of the heap may be left open, to allow of setting out, either in a pot or planted out in the earth, a choice specimen plant. Among the plants the most appropriate for the centre are: *Eulalia Japonica variegata*, and *Zebrina*. A variegated Agave may appropriately occupy the place, or some of the tall native wild ferns. A narrow circle may be cut around the base of the rockery, six or eight inches wide; after this is spaded up a row of blue Lobelia may be planted around the whole circle. Instead of the Lobelia, a row of *Echeveria secunda glauca*, or of the Mountain-of-Snow Geranium would look very finely. It may be well to mention here a number of the plants most appropriate for rockeries. Who is not familiar with the Moneywort, with its low-trailing habit and small yellow flowers? It is peculiarly adapted for rockeries. Portulaca, Paris Daisy (*Chrysanthemum frutescens*), *Myosotis* (Forget-me-not), are among the most popular plants for rockeries. The small Sedum or Stone Crop (*Sedum acre*), is an interesting and useful little plant, growing freely on rock or rustic work. As vines are much used for such places, we will mention as the best hardy vines for this purpose Veitch's *Ampelopsis* (*A. tricuspidata*), English or Irish Ivy, and the so-called running Myrtle. The above are entirely hardy and will stand any amount of freezing without injury.

The following vines, although not hardy, are much used for rockeries: Thunbergias, Tropæolums, Kenilworth Ivy, and the German Ivy (*Senecio scandens*). Where a rockery is formed in the midst of a pond of water, as is often done, plants of the kind mentioned will not flourish so well as those of a semi-aquatic nature, such as Caladiums, Callas, some Ferns, Cannas, and Lycopodiums, all of which will flourish in moist places.

CHAPTER XXVII.

BUDDING.

Budding as an art is simple, useful, and easily acquired by any one with a little practice. More can be learned practically about budding in a few hours spent with a skillful nurseryman while he is performing the operation, than could be derived from anything we might write on the subject. We are aware that we shall not be able to state in this brief chapter what will be new or instructive to experienced gardeners or nurserymen. This is not our aim, what may be old to them is likely to be new to thousands of amateur gardeners. In another part of this book will be found a chapter on grafting; this, though differently performed, is analogous in its results to budding, and many amateurs not infrequently speak of them in the same terms. To graft a cion, one end is carefully cut in the shape of a wedge, and inserted in a cleft where it is to grow; on the other hand, in budding, we use but a single eye, taken from a small branch, and insert it inside of the bark of the stock or tree we wish to bud. From this one eye, we may in time look for a tree laden with precious fruit. To be more explicit, and by way of illustration, we will imagine a seedling apple tree, a "natural," to have grown up in our garden. If left alone, the fruit of that seedling tree would probably be worthless, but we don't propose to risk that, and will proceed to bud it with some kind more worthy of room in a garden. When the proper season for budding fruit arrives, generally from the first to the latter part of July, will be the time to bud, if the stock is growing thriftily. A keen-bladed budding knife made for the purpose, a "cion" or "stick" of the variety to be budded, some twine (basswood bark is the best), make up the needed outfit for this operation. If the seedling is large, say five or six feet high, it should be top-budded, putting in a bud or two in each of the thriftiest branches. If the stock is not over one to two feet high, a single bud a few inches from the ground will be the best way to make a good tree of it. At the spot where we have decided to insert the bud, we will make a short, horizontal cut, then downwards a short, perpendicular "slit," not over an inch long, and just penetrating through the bark; open the slit, care being taken not to scratch the wood within, then insert the bud at the top of the cut, and slide it down to its proper place inside of the bark, the top of the bud being in juxtaposition with the horizontal cut above. Considerable skill is required to cut a bud properly, and two methods are practised, known as "budding with the wood in," and "budding with the wood out." The former consists in cutting a very little wood with the bud, a little deeper than the bark itself, and in the latter the wood is removed from the bud, leaving nothing but the bare bark. Unquestionably the surest way for a young budder is to remove the wood, cutting a pretty deep bud, and then in making the cross cut let it be only as deep as the bark, and by giving it a twitch the bud will readily leave the wood. I will say, however, that most nurserymen insist on budding with the wood, which it is claimed is the surest and best way to bud. We have tried both ways for years, and have been able to discover no difference, excepting where the buds are quite green at the time of budding, when it is best to have a little wood with the bud to sustain it. Plums should invariably be budded with the wood out.

After the bud has been properly set, it should be firmly tied with a broad string, making the laps close enough to entirely cover the slip, leaving the eye of the bud uncovered. Various kinds of strings for tying buds are used by nurserymen, but the basswood bark, which is made into broad, ribbon-like strips, seems peculiarly adapted for the purpose, and we advise its use where one has any considerable amount of budding to do. It usually takes from three to four weeks for a bud to callous and form a union with the stock; at the expiration of this time the strings should be taken off; we would except only those cases where the stock is growing, when if the strings pinch the stock too closely, they can be removed some time sooner.

The stock or stocks can now be left until the following spring, when the top should be cut away to within an inch or less of the bud; this will assist the roots to throw all their energy into the bud.

TOP-BUDDING TREES.

The top-budding of fruit and ornamental trees is much practised now-a-days by orchardists and fruit-growers generally, and sometimes with marked success.

A famous horticulturist of Geneva, N. Y., some years ago planted a large number of Lombard plum trees, which he fondly expected to see come into bearing while quite young, and be early compensated for his labor and expense in planting them. He waited a number of years without seeing his hopes realized; his patience at last became exhausted, and starting, lie top-budded them all with the Bradshaw plum, which grew rapidly, and bore abundantly in a couple of years, and last season he received eight dollars per bushel for the fruit in the Philadelphia market. It is a well known fact among fruit-growers that some rank-growing varieties of fruit trees, as for instance the Keiffer Hybrid Pear, do not produce fruit so early, or in such abundance as some less thrifty-growing varieties, such as the *Beurre Clairgeau*, but by top-budding the latter-named sort on to a thrifty specimen of the former, we have a tree that will bear fruit almost every year.

Nothing will take better from the bud than the rose; some elegant tree roses can be grown by simply training up a shoot of any common or wild rose to a sufficient hight, about five feet, and then top-budding it with three or four choice hybrids, as the *Gen. Jacqueminot, La Reine, Coquette des Alps*, and *Black Prince*, and those gems of the floral kingdom, when in blossom, will form a variety of dazzling beauties, the effect of which will not only be charming to the eye, but novel as well. I once removed from the door-yard a large rose bush of the *Crimson Boursault* variety, which had a number of large limbs on, into a corner of the conservatory, and there budded into it fifty different choice varieties of Roses of all classes: Hybrids, Teas, Noisettes, Bourbons, China, and Bengal varieties. The effect of all these different Roses, when in full blow the following summer was amazing; a perfect galaxy of the "Queen of Flowers."

A similar operation is possible for any skillful amateur florist to perform who has the facilities of a hot-house.

Budding can only be done when, ripe buds can be obtained, and when the stock to be budded is in a growing and thrifty condition, so that when opening the bark of the stock, the same peels freely, and opens readily at the touch of the knife. We will append here a brief table showing at what months of the summer different trees may be budded:

Apples   July 10th to 12th.

Pears	July 10th to 12th.
Plums	July 10th to 12th.
Cherries	July 20th to Aug. 1st.
Quinces	July 20th to Aug. 1st.
Peaches	July 20th to Aug. 1st.
Nectarines	Aug. 10th to 20th.
Apricots	Aug. 10th to 20th.

Most all sorts of ornamental trees, including Roses, in the ordinary season; namely, from July to August 1st.

CHAPTER XXVIII.

PRUNING.

If we plant trees or shrubs upon our grounds with the hope of making them more attractive, and at the same time indulge in the common and mistaken idea that, if we only plant them that nature will take care of their future, and grow them into handsome and shapely trees and shrubs—we labor in vain. It is not uncommon to see in the centre of refinement and culture every where, sadly neglected door-yards; these are filled with rampant bushes, and wide-spreading evergreens; such yards have more of a "cemetery look" than should belong to the surroundings of a cheerful home.

With a little pruning in the proper season, these unshapely bushes might become things of beauty, and not only look better, but will do better, if given a severe trimming in the spring. Hedges of Privet, Purple Barberry, and Japan Quince, look much prettier along the walk than the old-fashioned fences, which are now being rapidly done away with.

They should be kept pruned low as to not allow them to grow over two feet high.

The proper time for trimming hedges of all kinds is in mid-summer, after the shrubs have made a thrifty growth; we would advise an annual pruning in order to have the hedge looking finely.

It is a bad plan to allow a hedge of any kind, especially an evergreen one, to run a number of years without trimming. If a hedge is neglected so long, and then severely pruned, it will look stubby and shabby for a year or two after. With a pair of sharp hedge-shears, a person having a straight eye will make a good job of the trimming every time.

The spring is the time of the year in which to do the pruning of all kinds of plants, vines, and shrubs, that are out of doors, as they are then dormant. Some prefer to prune grape vines in the fall, just after they have ripened and shed their leaves. We think it unsafe to prune anything too severely in the fall, especially the grape vine. Much experience has taught us to select the month of March as the time of the year most suitable for performing the operation.

Every one who has a garden should possess a pruning knife with a long blade, curved at the end, for the operation. Armed with this implement, let us take a walk upon the lawn, and down into the garden, while the snow is still white upon the ground. The first thing that we meet as we enter the garden, is the large grape trellis, with its mass of tangled brown canes, a perfect mat of long vines and curling tendrils. How are we to attack this formidable network of vines in order to do anything with them? The first thing to be done is to sever all the cords and ties that fasten the vines to the trellis, and allow them to fall to the ground for convenience in trimming them. Spread the vines out full length upon the ground, and beginning at one of its arms, cut each shoot of the previous season's growth back to two eyes; if the canes are too numerous some may be cut out entirely. After all the "arms" of each vine have been pruned in this manner, the vine can be returned to the arbor and tied up as before. If there is a prospect of cold weather let the vines lie upon the ground, as they will be less liable to "bleed," or to suffer from the cold. This is the simplest way we know of to trim grape vines, and any amateur gardener can do it if he tries this manner. Walking a little further, we come upon some rose bushes: there are too many branches among them, and too much old wood, and some that is entirely dead. With our knife we will remove at least one half of this excess of wood, leaving as much young wood of the previous season's growth as possible by thinning out the old limbs and dead wood severely. Here is one Moss Rose bush, the stems appear as brown and looking as seared as a berry; it is apparently winter killed, and by cutting into it we find that to be the case; the roots are in all probability sound, and we will cut the stems down to the ground and cover the place with a forkful of stable manure; if the roots are alive it will grow and bloom the coming summer. Here is a large standard Rose with a fine top, we will head this back short, cutting each stem to an eye or two of the bottom. Proceeding to the lawn we run across some weeping deciduous trees, among them is a large Kilmarnock Weeping Willow, its beautiful pendant branches fairly reach the ground, and switch the snow as they sway to and fro. Nothing more beautiful could be imagined. We would head this back close, and it should be done every spring and most of the old wood thinned out. This large climbing Rose that clings so close to the piazza, should be trimmed about in the same way as we did the grape vine, and also this large Clematis Jackmanii should be cut to the ground and allowed to start up anew in the spring. Here is a clump of shrubbery among which we see the *Weigela, Spiræas, Purple Fringe, Deutzia crenata, Hydrangea paniculata grandiflora,* the Syringa, and a number of other favorite shrubs. These will all need more or less cutting back and trimming, and now is a good time to do it. We know one gentleman who boasted the finest display of Roses in his county, who was in the habit of cutting his Rose bushes down to the ground every spring, and when they began to grow he had dug in around each one an abundance of well rotted compost, "and," said he, "I have never seen the day, from June to October, that I could not pluck a large bouquet of the choicest Hybrid Perpetual roses, while my next door neighbor, who also had rose bushes, could find no flower after June." I will say that this gentleman was in the habit of cutting his roses once a day, and never allowing the flowers to fade on the bush, which is an excellent plan to keep up a perpetuity of bloom.

CHAPTER XXIX.

MISCELLANEOUS NOTES.

TREE ROSES.

In planting tree roses received from the nursery or elsewhere, be sure and set them deep; the stem, for six or eight inches above the collar, should be under ground. If wet moss be tied about the stem and head of the tree after it has been planted, and the moss kept wet for a week or two after planting, or until the buds begin to start, it will, in nine cases out of ten, save the tree. The moss maybe removed after the growth begins. If planted in the fall, the body and top should be well wrapped up in straw.

THE LAWN.

If one has a fine lawn and desires to keep it so, he should never work upon or mow it when the turf is wet or soggy. The impression made by the feet in walking over the sod while in this state, will leave the surface rough and uneven afterwards. Do not water the grass or plants while the sun is shining hot, as it will scorch the leaves and make them turn yellow. All weeds, such as dandelions, plantain, etc., growing up through the grass, should be carefully and thoroughly dug out by the roots with a knife or pointed spade; if allowed to remain, they will soon become so numerous as eventually to kill out the grass and give to the lawn an appearance of neglect.

LAWN VASES.

The earth in vases of plants that stand out in exposed places, will rapidly dry out; if shells or fine gravel is laid over the surface of the soil, they will prevent it from "baking" after watering, and hold the moisture much longer than without. Try it.

PLANTING TREES.

The spring is preferable to the fall for setting out trees and shrubs of all kinds. In the Northern States they should be set out about the first of April, to give the roots time enough to become established before warm weather starts the leaves.

Of thousands of trees and shrubs that we have planted at this season, comparatively few failed to live and grow, providing they were in good condition at the time of planting. Young trees should not be headed back the year they are set out, but the roots may be trimmed a little, cutting off all that are bruised and broken. The hole in which a tree or shrub is to be set, should be ample enough to receive all the roots without cramping them into a ball, as is the habit of some who plant trees, the soil filled in about the roots should be fine, but not the sub-soil, which should be replaced by richer earth. Never allow manure to come in direct contact with the roots at the time of planting. It is very injurious, but it may be applied on the surface as a mulch, with safety.

BOTANICAL NAMES.

All species of plants belong to some particular genus, and bear a botanical, as well as a common name, by which they are distinguished. Those who have studied botany will know the exact botanical name of the plants in most collections. We sometimes see persons making themselves ridiculous by a pretended display of knowledge on matters of horticulture and botany, giving or pretending to give the botanical name of every plant one may happen to mention. The following anecdote will apply to such: Mr. Sidney Smith, the famous English writer, was once visiting the conservatory of a young lady who was proud of her plants and flowers, and used (not very accurately) a profusion of botanical names. "Madam," he said, "have you the *Psoriasis septennis*?" "No," she said, very innocently, "I had it last winter, and I gave it to the Archbishop of Canterbury, and it came out beautifully in the spring." *Psoriasis septennis*, is the medical name for the "Seven year Itch!"

FROZEN PLANTS.

Tender plants that have become frozen, or but slightly touched by frost, can be saved, if taken before they commence to thaw out; sprinkle or dip the affected part in cold water, and then remove the plant or plants into a dark place to remain for a day, then bring them to the light. We have saved whole beds of tender plants from death by early frosts in the autumn, by getting up long before sunrise, drenching the leaves with water, and then covering the plants with a sheet or blanket.

CUTTING GRASS.

It is so easy to mow the lawn with the light-running modern lawn-mower, that many fine lawns are injured by too frequent mowings. We should not follow any set time for mowing, but be governed by the growth of the grass and the weather. When hot weather approaches, the grass should be cut less often, for too close cutting will expose the roots, and if the weather be dry and hot for a considerable period, the grass as a consequence will wither prematurely.

AN ARCH.

A very simple thing sometimes will look the most attractive. By driving two limber poles into the ground by the side of each of two gate posts, and bringing the two ends of the poles together, and fasten them securely, a respectable arch can be made. At the foot of each pole plant a *Clematis Jackmanii*, and train them to run up their poles; they will grow rapidly, and in a short time the arch will be covered with beautiful purple stars. This Clematis is entirely hardy, and can be used for the same purpose every year by cutting it close to the ground in the fall when done growing.

BLOOM.

When watering plants avoid wetting the foliage as much as possible, as they will not bloom as freely as if the leaves were dry. Geraniums are known to bloom a great deal more freely where the roots are confined to a small space, and the soil about them kept rather dry; especially is this so with the double sorts.

Geraniums may be grafted successfully; the short growers, like Mrs. Pollock, Mountain of Snow, and Happy Thought, can be top-grafted on to the strong-growing kinds, like Gen. Grant, Madam Lemoine, and other strong-growers. If half a dozen sorts are grafted on a single stock, they will, when in bloom, appear as a curiosity.

MILDEW.

Mildew is a microscopic fungus, that is parasitic upon cultivated plants. Roses, Bouvardias, and especially grape vines, are subject to its attacks. If not arrested, mildew will soon strip a plant of its foliage. Whenever a whitish dust, as if flour had been sprinkled upon them, appears upon the leaves, particularly those of the Rose, and its leaves curl up, it is evident that the plant is attacked by mildew, and some remedy must be at once applied to prevent the spread of the trouble. Several excellent remedies are used by florists and gardeners for the prevention and cure of mildew. None of these are more effective than the following, which, if applied in time, before the disease has become so bad as to be beyond help, will very surely arrest it. Take three pounds each, of Flowers of Sulphur and Quick-lime, put these together and add sufficient hot water to slake the lime. When the lime is slaked, add six gallons of water, and boil down to two gallons. Allow the lime to settle, and pour off the clear liquid and bottle it for use. To treat plants affected by mildew, add one gill of the liquid, prepared as above, to six gallons of water, and mix well together. This is to be freely syringed upon the plants every other day. It will not only arrest mildew, but prevent it. Sudden changes of temperature, as cool nights following warm days, tend to the production of mildew, and with house plants, these sudden changes should be carefully guarded against.

CHAPTER XXX.

SENTIMENT AND LANGUAGE OF FLOWERS.

Amaranth	Immortality.
Amaryllis	Beautiful, but timid.
Aster, double	Variety.
Aster, German	Afterthought.
Arbutus	Thee only do I love.
Acacia	Friendship.
Apple Blossom	Preference.
Asphodel	Remembered after death.
Arbor Vitæ	Unchanging friendship.
Alyssum	Worth beyond beauty.
Anemone	Your love changes.
Azalea	Pleasant recollections.
Argeratum	Worth beyond beauty.
Balsam	Impatience.
Blue Bell	Constancy.
Balm	Pleasantry.
Bay-leaf	I change but in death.
Bachelor's Button	Hope.
Begonia	Deformed.
Bitter Sweet	Truth.
Buttercup	Memories of childhood.
Brier, Sweet	Envy.
Calla	Feminine Modesty.
Carnation	Pride.
Clematis	Mental Excellence.
Cypress	Disappointment, Despair

Crocus	Happiness.
Columbine	I cannot give thee up.
Cresses	Always cheerful.
Canterbury Bell	Constancy.
Cereus, Night-blooming	Transient beauty.
Candytuft	Indifference.
Chrysanthemum	Heart left desolate.
Clover, White	I promise.
Clover, Four-leaved	Be mine.
Crown Imperial	Authority.
Camellia	Spotless purity.
Cissus	Changeable.
Centaurea	Your looks deceive me.
Cineraria	Singleness of heart.
Daisy, Field	I will think of it.
Dahlia	Dignity.
Daffodil	Unrequited love.
Dandelion	Coquetry.
Everlasting	Always remembered.
Everlasting Pea	Wilt thou go with me.
Ebony	Blackness.
Fuchsia	Humble love.
Foxglove	Insincerity.
Fern	Sincerity.
Fennel	Strength.
Forget-me-not	For ever remembered.
Fraxinella	Fire.
Geranium, Ivy	Fond of dancing.
Geranium, Oak	A melancholy mind.
Geranium, Rose	I prefer you.

Geranium, Scarlet	Stillness.
Gladiolus	Ready armed.
Golden Rod	Encouragement.
Gillyflower	Promptness.
Hyacinth	Benevolence.
Honeysuckle	Devoted love.
House Leek	Domestic economy.
Heliotrope	I adore you.
Hibiscus	Delicate beauty.
Hollyhock	Ambition.
Hydrangea	Vain glory.
Ice Plant	Your looks freeze me.
Ivy	Friendship.
Iris, German	Flame.
Iris, Common Garden	A message for thee.
Jonquil	Affection returned.
Jessamine, White	Amiability.
Jessamine, Yellow	Gracefulness.
Larkspur	Fickleness.
Lantana	Rigor.
Laurel	Words though sweet may deceive.
Lavender	Mistrust.
Lemon Blossom	Discretion.
Lady Slipper	Capricious beauty.
Lily of the Valley	Return of happiness.
Lilac, White	Youth.
Lilac, Blue	First emotions of love.
Lily, Water	Eloquence.
May Flower	Welcome.
Marigold	Sacred affection.

Marigold and Cypress	Despair.
Mandrake	Rarity.
Mignonette	Your qualities surpass your charms.
Morning Glory	Coquetry, Affectation.
Mock Orange	Counterfeit.
Myrtle	Love in absence.
Mistletoe	Insurmountable.
Narcissus	Egotism.
Nasturtium	Patriotism.
Oxalis	Reverie.
Orange Blossom	Purity.
Olive	Peace.
Oleander	Beware.
Primrose	Modest worth.
Pink, White	Pure love.
Pink, Red	Devoted love.
Phlox	Our hearts are united.
Periwinkle	Sweet memories.
Pæony	Ostentation.
Pansy	You occupy my thoughts.
Poppy	Oblivion.
Rhododendron	Agitation.
Rose, Bud	Confession of love.
Rose, Bud White	Too young to love.
Rose, Austrian	Thou art all that is lovely.
Rose, Leaf	I never trouble.
Rose, Monthly	Beauty ever new.
Rose, Moss	Superior merit.
Rose, Red	I love you.
Rose, Yellow	Infidelity.

Rosemary	Remembrance.
Sensitive Plant	Modesty.
Snow-Ball	Thoughts in heaven.
Snow-Drop	Consolation.
Sumach	Pride and poverty.
Sweet William	Gallantry.
Syringa	Memory.
Sunflower	Lofty thought.
Tuberose	Purity of mind.
Thyme	Activity.
Tulip, var	Beautiful eyes.
Tulip, Red	Declaration of love.
Tritoma	Fiery temper.
Verbena, Sensibility.	
Verbena, Purple	I weep for you.
Verbena, White	Pray for me.
Violet, Blue	Faithfulness.
Violet, White	Purity, candor.
Woodbine	Fraternal love.
Wall Flower	Fidelity in misfortune.
Wistaria	Close friendship.
Wax Plant	Artificial beauty.
Yucca	Your looks pierce me.
Yew	Sadness.
Zinnia	I mourn your absence.

www.ingramcontent.com/pod-product-compliance
Lightning Source LLC
Chambersburg PA
CBHW080022110526
44587CB00021BA/3740